NOW YOU CAN READ....
SAMUEL

STORY RETOLD BY ELAINE IFE

ILLUSTRATED BY RUSSELL LEE

Published by Rourke Publications, Inc. P.O. Box 868,
Windermere, Florida 32786. Copyright © 1983 by Rourke
Publications, Inc. All copyrights reserved. No part of this
book may be reproduced in any form without written per-
mission from the publisher. Printed in the United States of
America.
   The Publishers acknowledge permission from Brimax
Books for the use of the name "Now You Can Read" and
"Large Type For First Readers" which identify Brimax Now
You Can Read series.

Library of Congress Cataloging in Publication Data

Ife, Elaine, 1955-
   Samuel.

   (Now you can read—Bible stories)
   Summary: Briefly retells the story of Samuel whose
mother gave him back to God, as she had promised, when
he was five years old.
   1. Samuel (Biblical judge)—Juvenile literature.
2. Bible.   O.T.—Biography—Juvenile literature.   3. Bible
stories, English—O.T. Samuel, 1st.   [1. Samuel (Biblical
judge)   2. Bible stories—O.T.]   I. Lee, Russell,
1944-   ill.   II. Title.   III. Series.
BS551.2.I35   1983   222'.43'0924 [B]   83-13752
ISBN 0-86625-222-3

GROLIER ENTERPRISES CORP.

NOW YOU CAN READ....
SAMUEL

One day, in a place called Shiloh,
the people took their children to
pray in God's house. It was called
the Temple.

The Temple was a holy place. Inside was an altar of wood and a shining lamp. Behind the altar, a tent hid the Ark of God. Inside, lay the holy laws God had given to the people.

When the people came out of the Temple, they had a great feast.

The children sang and had a happy time.

One woman, whose name was Hannah, sat alone. She had no children. She wished that she could have just one child. Year after year she waited. No child was born. Hannah was very sad.

She left the feast and walked back to the Temple. At the door, sat the old priest Eli. Hannah walked past him and knelt down.

She prayed to God. She asked Him to send her a baby. "If I have a son," she said, "I will give him back to you. He will do your work."

Eli went up to her and said,
"What is the matter?"
She told him and he said,
"Go in peace. May God give you
what you want."
Hannah felt happy as she went back
to the feast.
Very soon, God gave Hannah a little
son. She called him Samuel.

She did not forget her promise to God. When Samuel was five years old, she made him a little coat. She took him with her to the Temple.

She went to Eli and said,

"I am the woman who asked God for a son. God has heard my prayer. This is the boy He sent me. Now I am giving him back to God as I promised."

Samuel was a good boy. Eli looked after him as if he were his own.

Every year, his mother went to see him. She took him a new coat.

Samuel helped Eli each day in the Temple.

Eli had two sons.
They did not help
him. They made
fun of holy things
and spent their
time in Shiloh.
Eli knew that his
sons did wicked
things, but he
said nothing.

Eli was very old
and nearly blind.
Samuel led Eli
everywhere.

Samuel slept in a corner of the Temple, near the lamp of gold. He had to see that the lamp was always kept burning. Samuel kept the oil ready.

One night, he woke up. He heard a voice calling "Samuel, Samuel." He thought it was Eli calling him. He ran through the Temple to where Eli lay. "I did not call you," Eli said. "Go back to sleep."

Again the voice called and once again, Samuel ran to Eli.
"I did not call you," said Eli.

When the voice called a third time, Eli knew that it was God who spoke to the boy. He said, "If you hear the voice again, you must say, 'Speak, Lord, I can hear you'."

Samuel did as Eli told him. He was not afraid. He waited. All was still in the Temple. The lamp glowed softly. God spoke to Samuel and said, "The sons of Eli are very wicked. Eli knows this. I shall punish Eli and his sons. You must tell Eli what I have said."

Samuel was sad. He loved Eli. He did not want to tell him what God had said.

Samuel could not sleep. He walked outside the Temple until the morning.

Then, as Eli sat under a great
tree outside the Temple, Samuel told
him God's words. Eli put his hands
over his face.
"God will do what is right," he
said at last.

At night in the Temple, God spoke many times to Samuel. People came from far away to hear Samuel. He told the people what God wanted them to do.

The years went by and war broke out. The people sent a message to the Temple. They wanted the Ark. They thought that God would help them if they carried it.

Eli's wicked sons took the Ark from the Temple

The Ark was carried into battle.

The Ark was taken by the enemy.
Eli's sons were killed in the
battle.

A man who had been in the fighting came to tell Eli about the battle. He found Eli sitting outside the Temple.

When Eli heard that the Ark of God had been taken, he died. The old man's heart was broken.

Samuel prayed to God to help the people. He told them to serve God. The people listened to Samuel for he spoke the word of God.

All these appear in the pages of
the story. Can you find them?

Temple

Ark

lamp

children

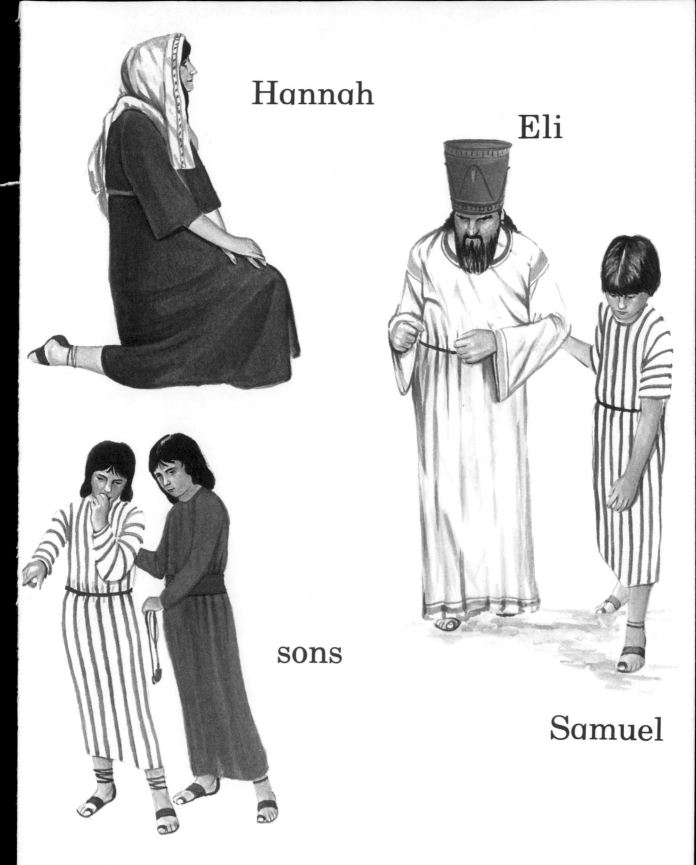

Hannah

Eli

sons

Samuel

Now tell the story in your own words.